JOSEPH MIDTHUN   SAMUEL HITI

BUILDING BLOCKS OF SCIENCE

THE SKELETAL AND MUSCULAR SYSTEMS

WORLD BOOK

a Scott Fetzer company
Chicago

www.worldbook.com

World Book, Inc.
180 North LaSalle Street
Suite 900
Chicago, Illinois 60601
USA

For information about other World Book publications,
visit our website at www.worldbook.com
or call 1-800-WORLDBK (967-5325).
For information about sales to schools and libraries,
call 1-800-975-3250 (United States),
or 1-800-837-5365 (Canada).

Library of Congress Cataloging-in-Publication Data

The skeletal and muscular systems.
        pages cm. --   (Building blocks of science)
    Includes index.
    Summary: "A graphic nonfiction volume that
introduces the skeletal and muscular systems
of the human body"-- Provided by publisher.
    ISBN 978-0-7166-1848-5
    1. Musculoskeletal system--Juvenile literature.
2. Human skeleton--Juvenile literature. I. World
Book, Inc.
    QP301.S58 2014
    611'.7--dc23
                                2013023500

Building Blocks of Science
ISBN: 978-0-7166-1840-9 (set, hc.)

Also available as:
ISBN: 978-0-7166-7875-5 (pbk.)
ISBN: 978-0-7166-7867-0 (trade, hc.)
ISBN: 978-0-7166-2958-0 (e-book, EPUB3)

Printed in China by Shenzhen Donnelley
Printing Co., Ltd., Guangdong Province
4th printing April 2017

STAFF

Executive Committee
President: Jim O'Rourke
Vice President and Editor in Chief:
    Paul A. Kobasa
Vice President, Finance: Donald D. Keller
Vice President, Marketing: Jean Lin
Vice President, International Sales:
    Maksim Rutenberg
Director, Human Resources: Bev Ecker

Editorial
Director, Digital & Print Content Development:
    Emily Kline
Senior Editor: Nicholas Kilzer
Editor, Digital & Print Content Development:
    Kendra Muntz
Manager, Indexing Services: David Pofelski
Manager, Contracts & Compliance
    (Rights & Permissions): Loranne K. Shields
Writer and Letterer: Joseph Midthun

Digital
Director, Digital Product Development:
    Erika Meller
Digital Product Manager: Jonathan Wills

Graphics and Design
Senior Art Director: Tom Evans
Coordinator, Design Development and
    Production: Brenda B. Tropinski
Book Design: Samuel Hiti

Manufacturing/Pre-Press
Manufacturing Manager: Anne Fritzinger
Proofreader: Nathalie Strassheim

Acknowledgments:
Created by Samuel Hiti and Joseph Midthun
Art by Samuel Hiti
Text by Joseph Midthun
Special thanks to Syril McNally

TABLE OF CONTENTS

There is a glossary on page 30. Terms defined in the glossary are in type **that looks like this** on their first appearance.

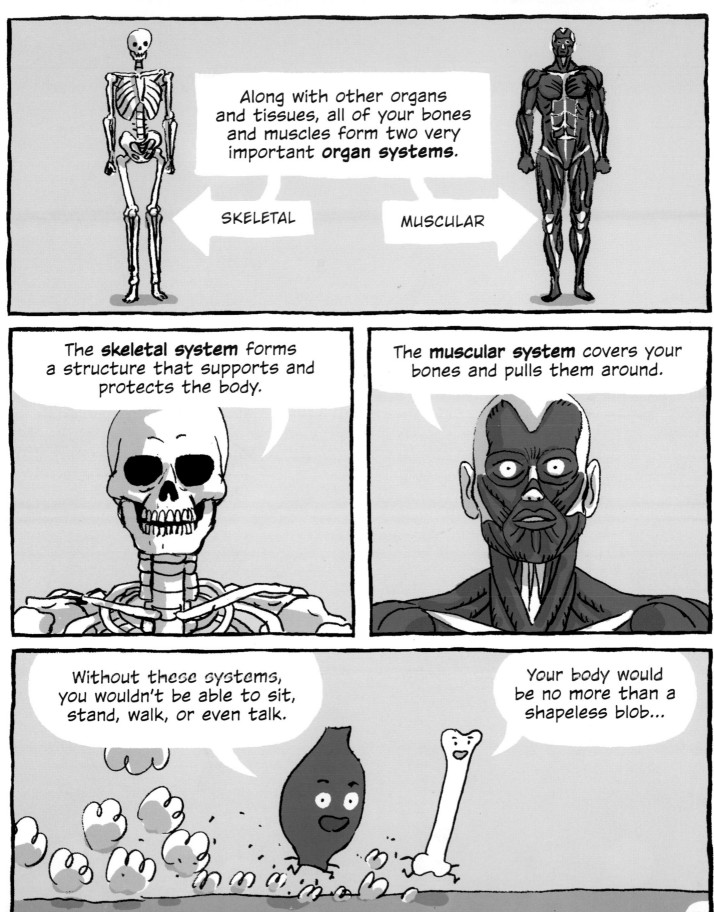

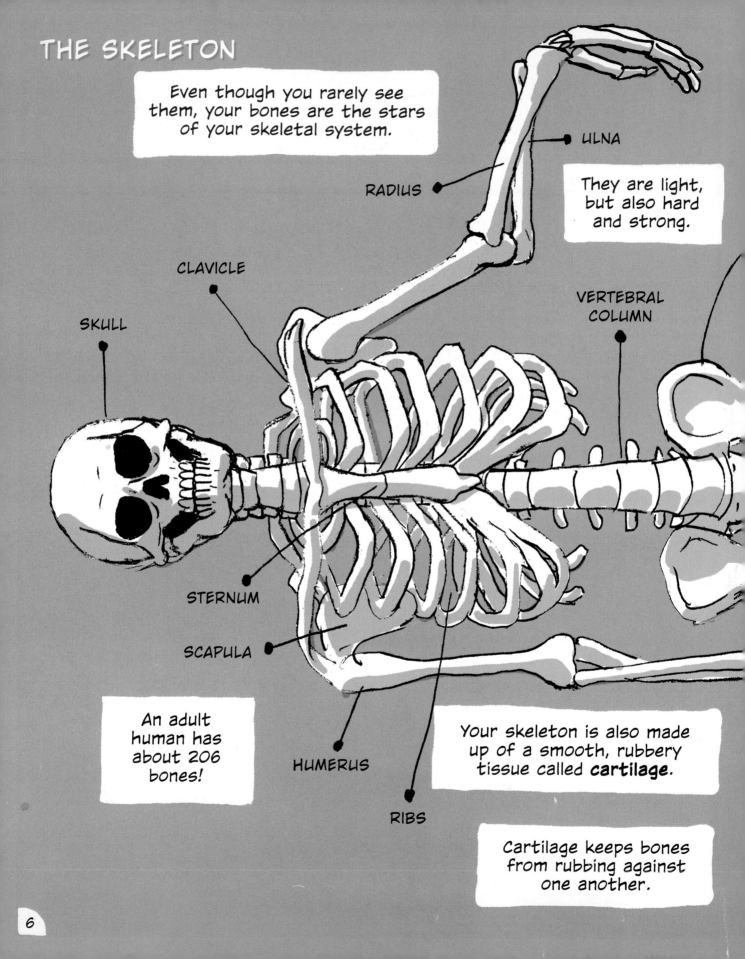

THE SKELETON

Even though you rarely see them, your bones are the stars of your skeletal system.

ULNA

They are light, but also hard and strong.

RADIUS

CLAVICLE

VERTEBRAL COLUMN

SKULL

An adult human has about 206 bones!

STERNUM

SCAPULA

HUMERUS

RIBS

Your skeleton is also made up of a smooth, rubbery tissue called **cartilage**.

Cartilage keeps bones from rubbing against one another.

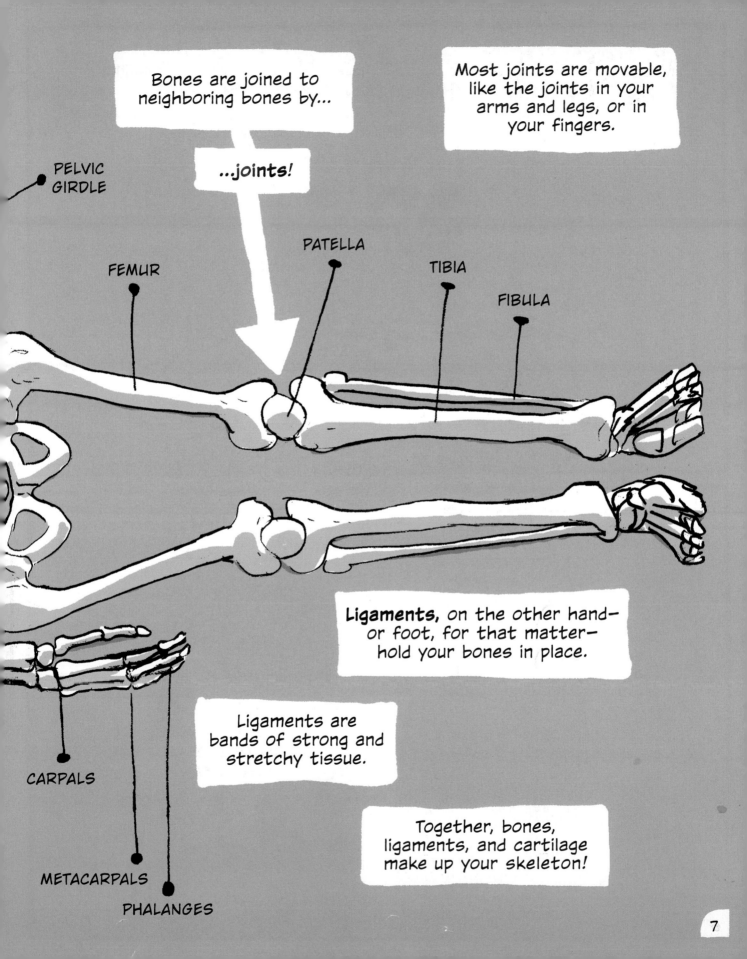

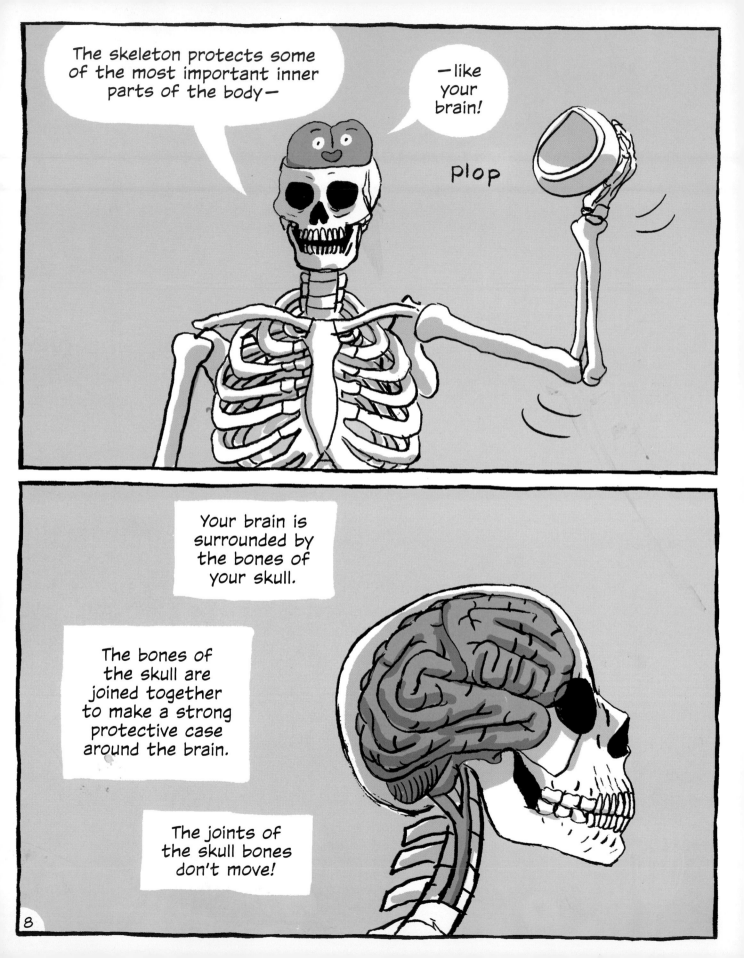

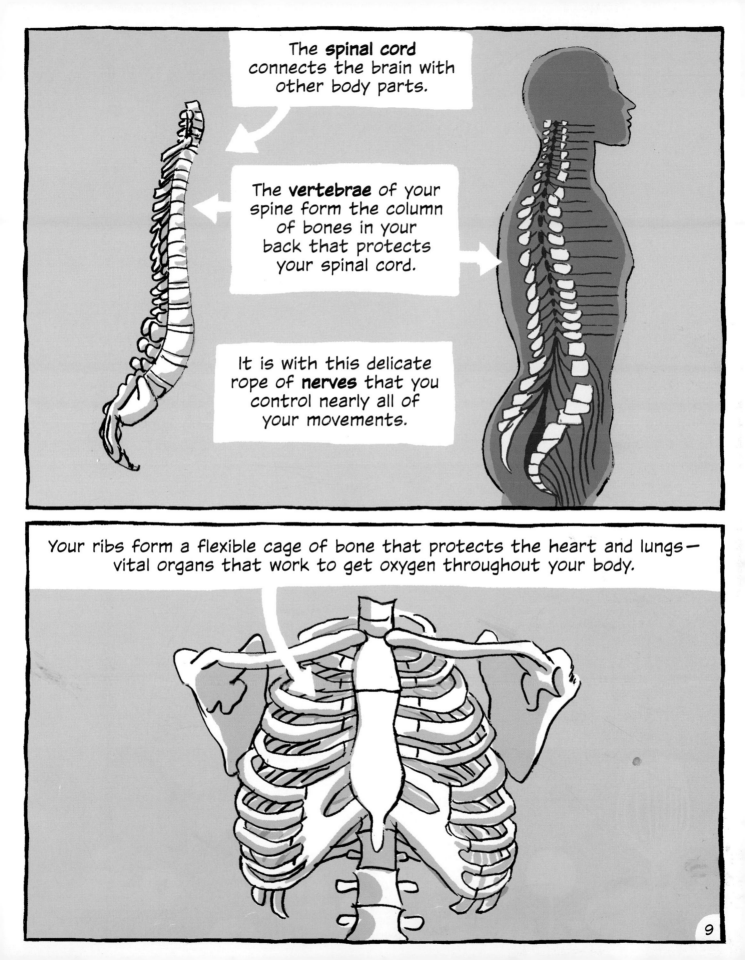

The **spinal cord** connects the brain with other body parts.

The **vertebrae** of your spine form the column of bones in your back that protects your spinal cord.

It is with this delicate rope of **nerves** that you control nearly all of your movements.

Your ribs form a flexible cage of bone that protects the heart and lungs—vital organs that work to get oxygen throughout your body.

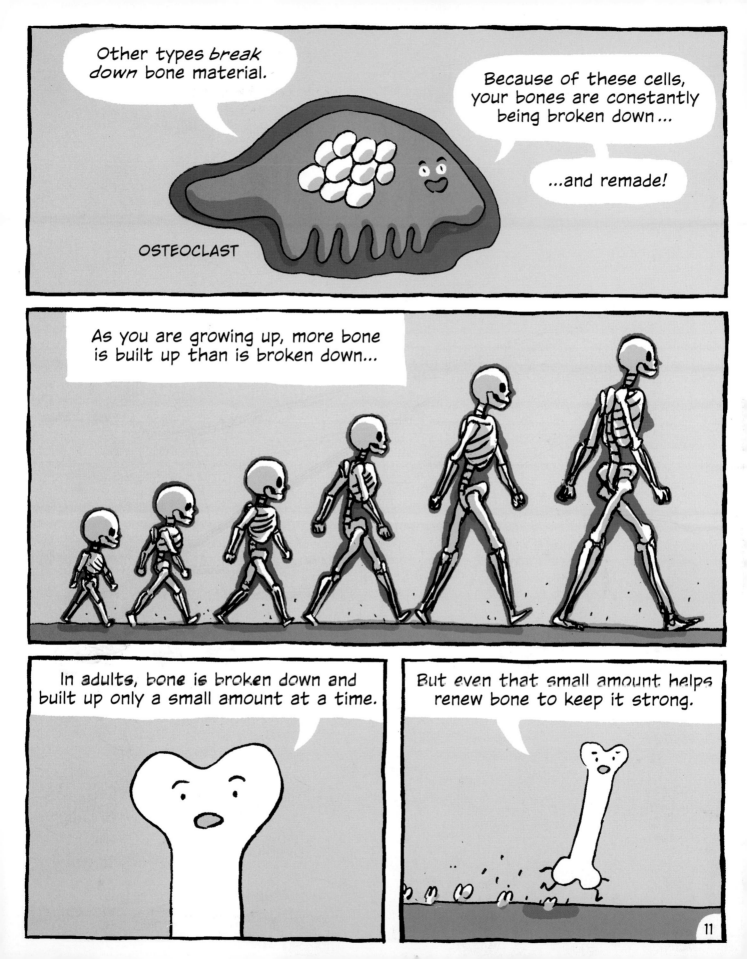

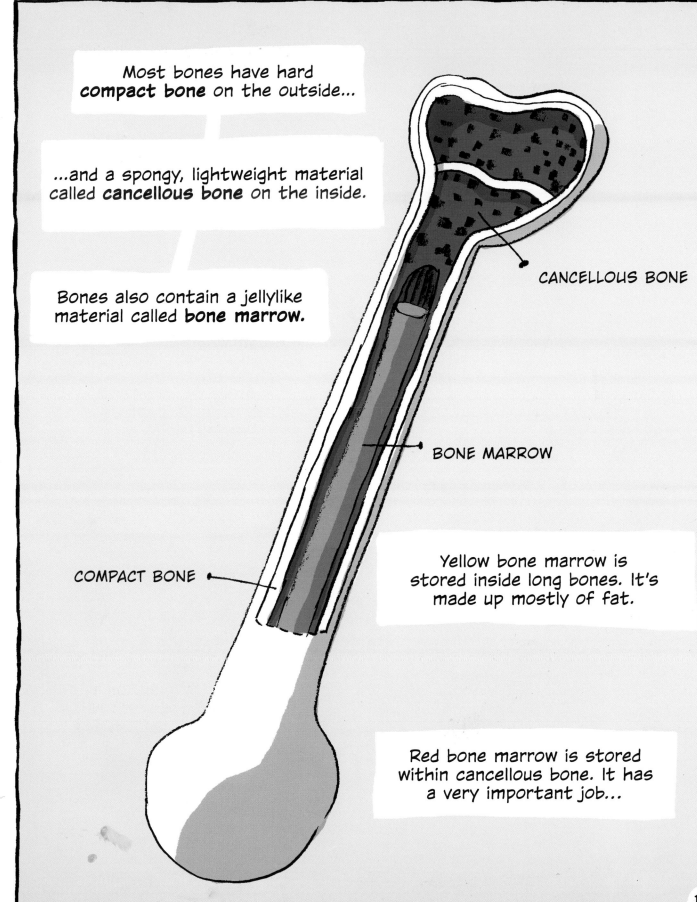

Most bones have hard **compact bone** on the outside...

...and a spongy, lightweight material called **cancellous bone** on the inside.

Bones also contain a jellylike material called **bone marrow.**

CANCELLOUS BONE

BONE MARROW

COMPACT BONE

Yellow bone marrow is stored inside long bones. It's made up mostly of fat.

Red bone marrow is stored within cancellous bone. It has a very important job...

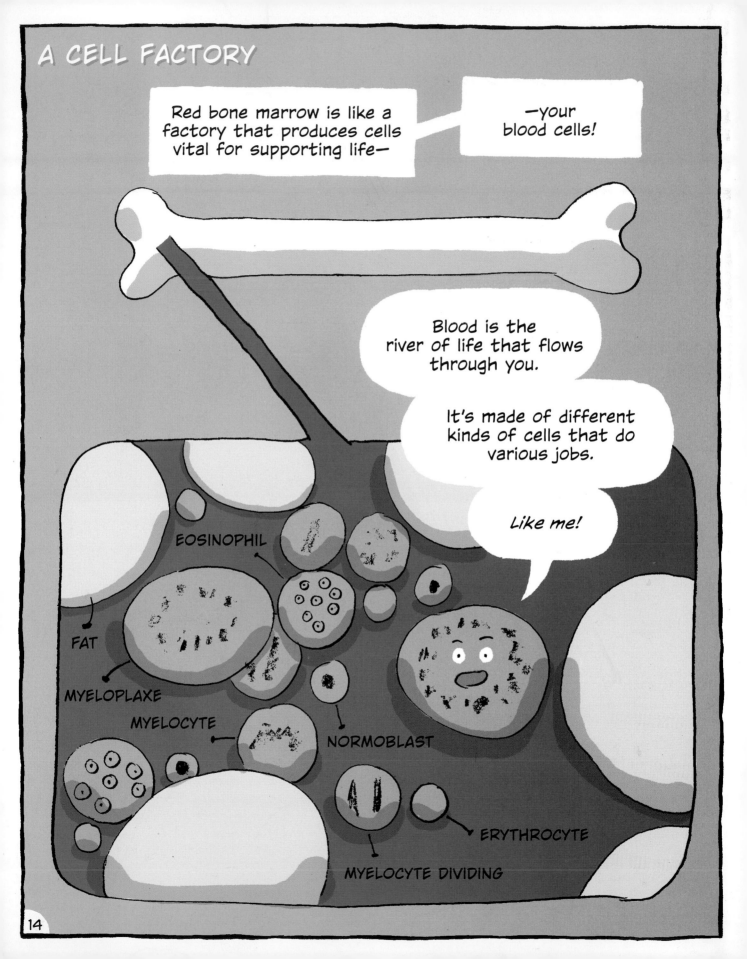

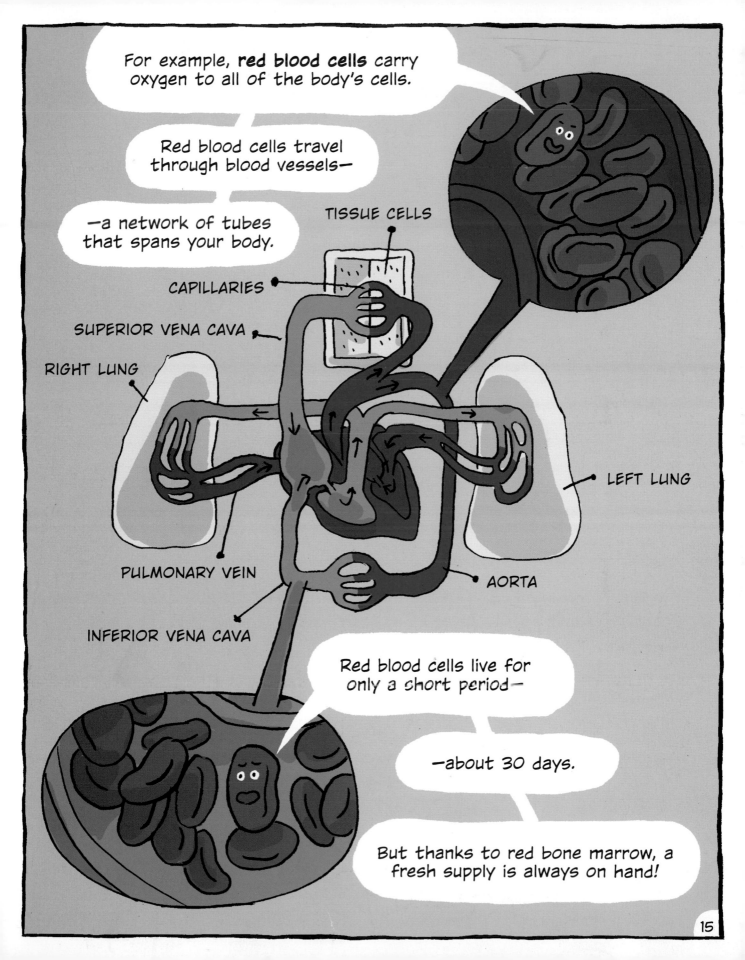

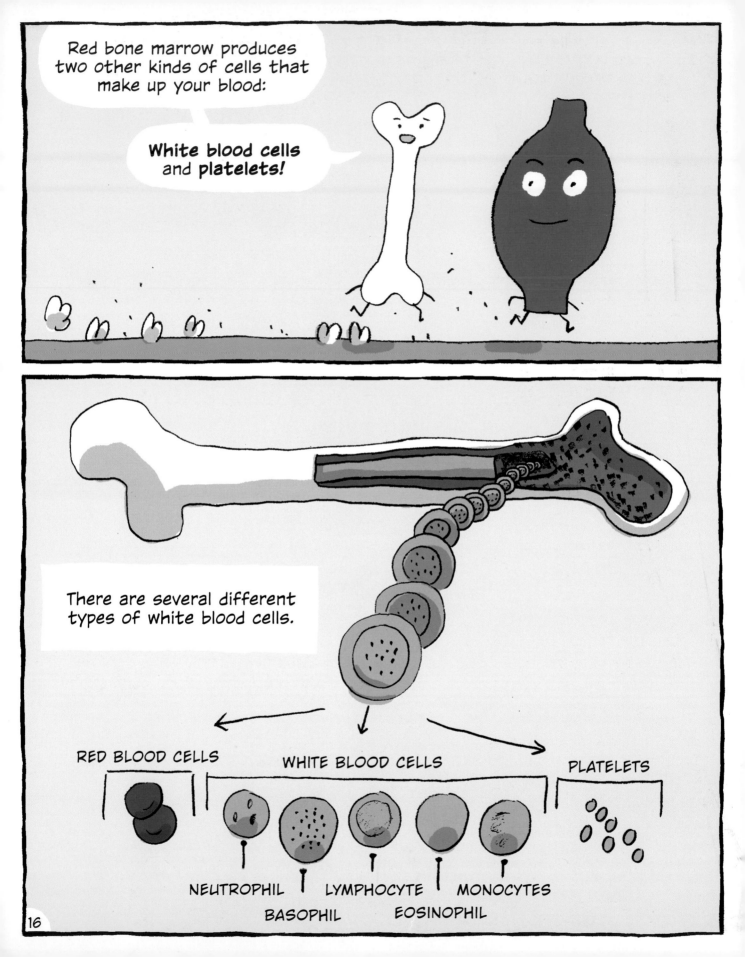

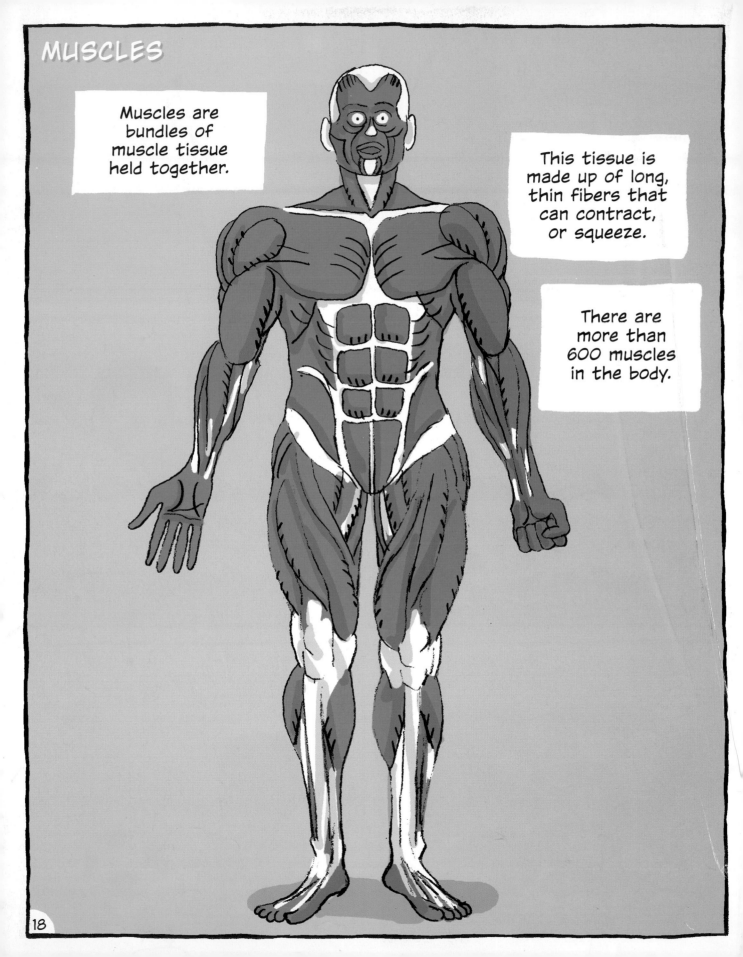

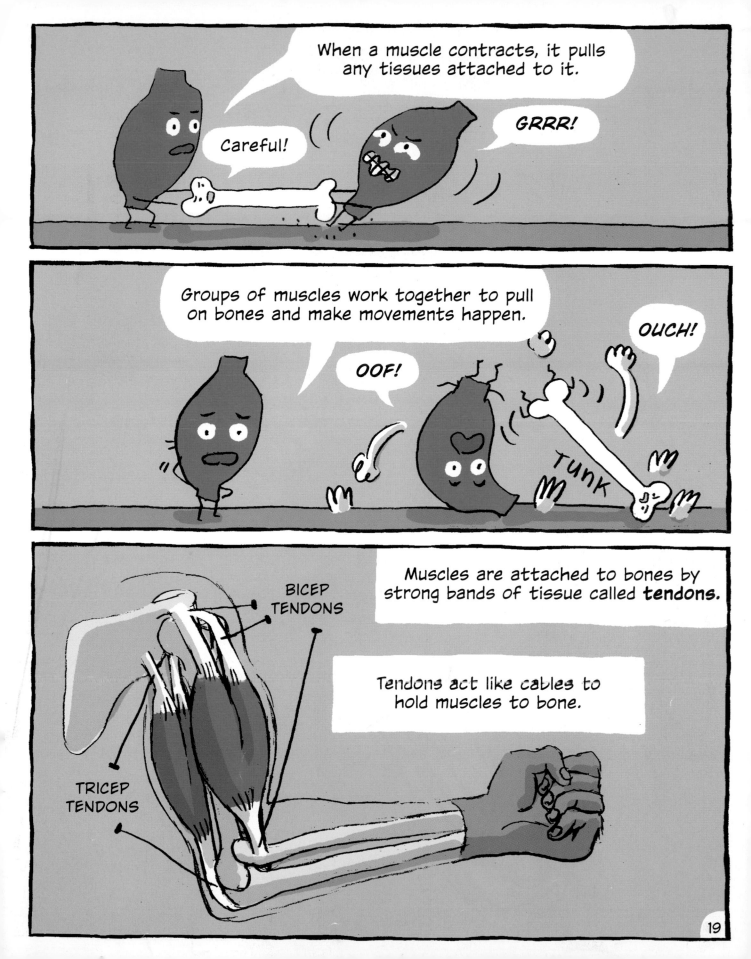

TYPES OF MUSCLES

There are three types of muscles.

Each type moves in a different way.

Skeletal muscle is muscle tissue attached to bones that works in pairs.

SMOOTH MUSCLE

CARDIAC MUSCLE

SKELETAL MUSCLE

It moves the bones of your arms, legs, fingers, and other body parts.

For example, when you raise your arm, one set of muscles contracts.

BICEP CONTRACTED

It pulls on the top side of your arm bones, lifting the arm up.

When these muscles relax, an opposite set of muscles pulls at the bones of your arm, your shoulder, and your back ...

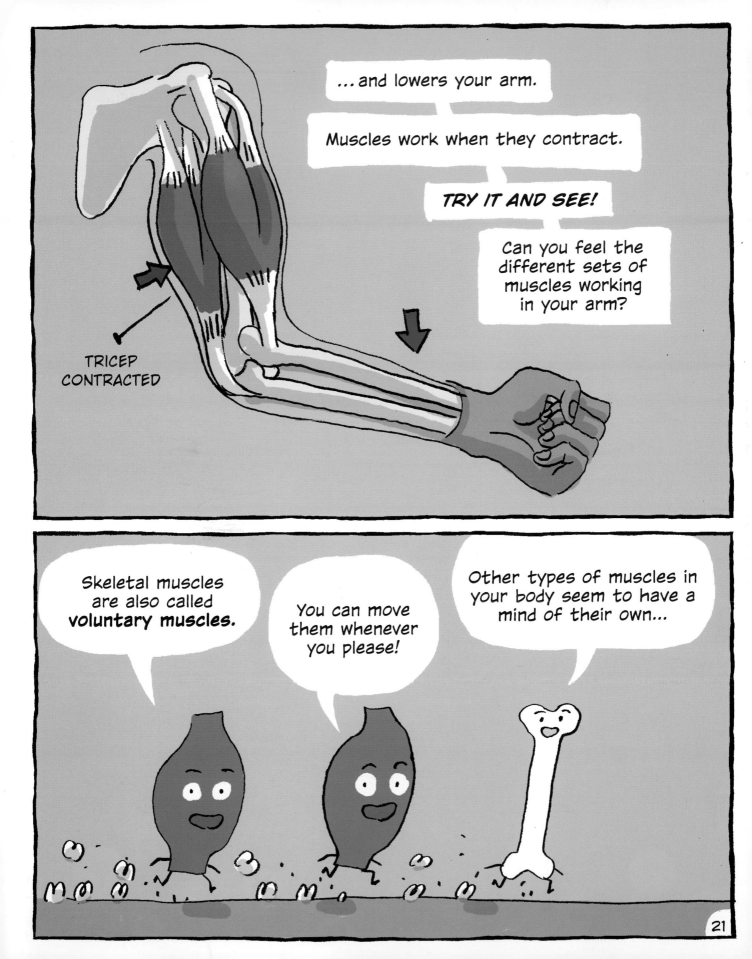

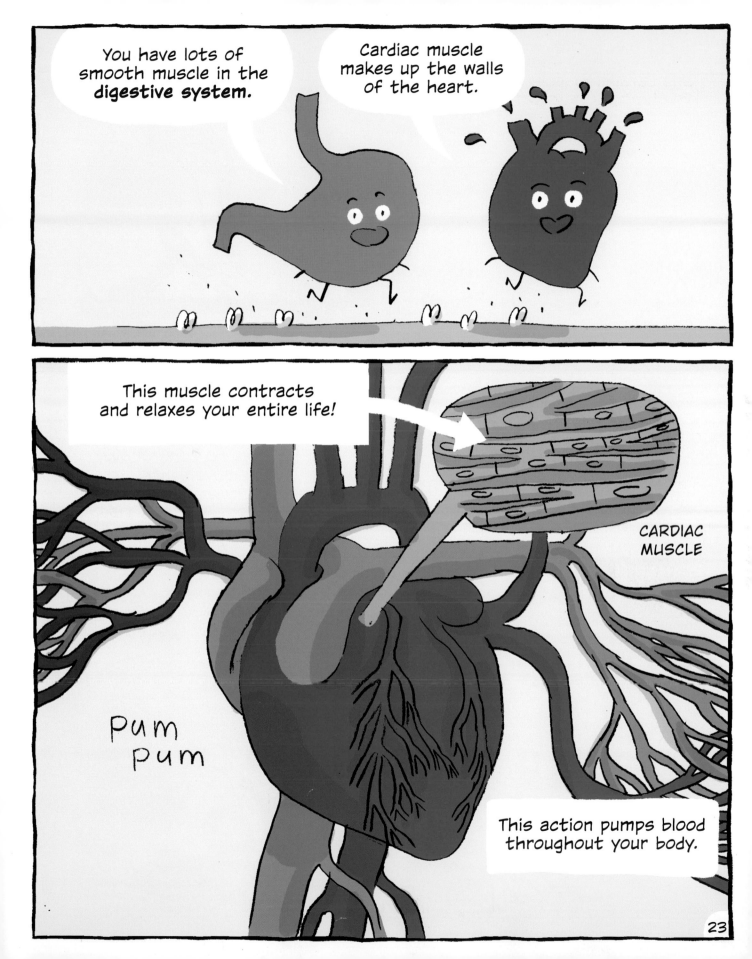

The nervous system is made up of bundles of fibers called nerves.

The nerves form a network of pathways in the body.

The pathways carry signals back and forth through the body.

This allows the brain to plan your movements and send instructions to the correct muscles to make movements happen.

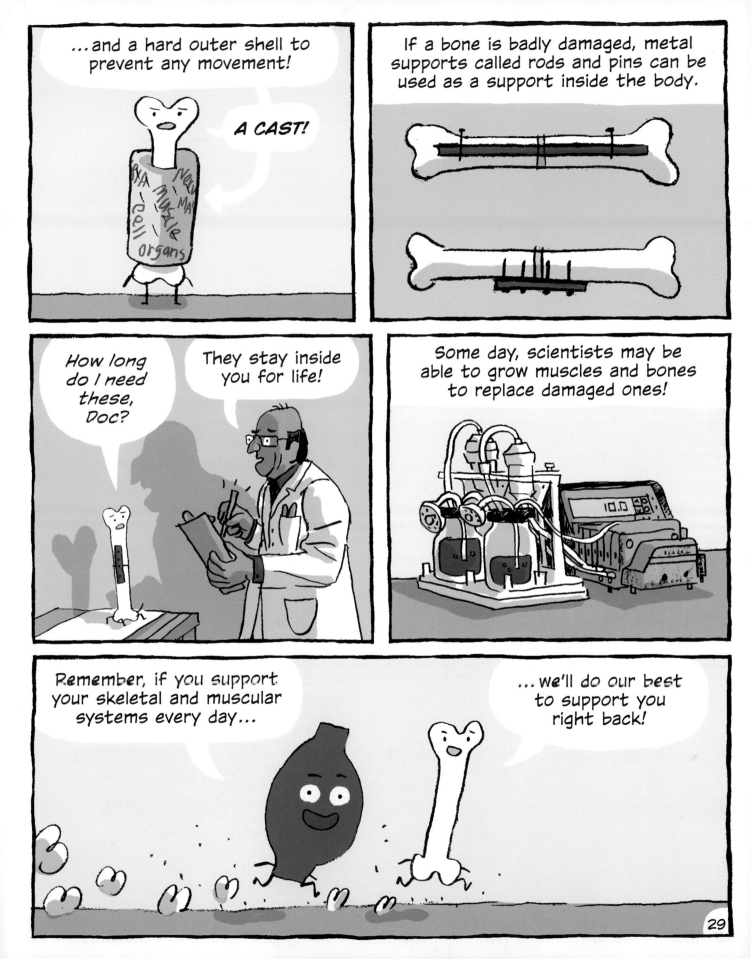

GLOSSARY

bacterium; bacteria a tiny single-celled organism; more than one bacterium.

blood vessel a hollow tube that carries blood and nutrients through the body.

bone marrow the soft center of bones that makes new blood cells.

cancellous bone the spongy, honeycombed material inside a bone.

cartilage smooth tissue at the end of bones.

cell the basic unit of all living things.

compact bone the solid outer part of a bone.

digestive system the group of organs that breaks down and absorbs food in the body.

involuntary muscle a muscle that cannot be controlled by thinking.

joint the places where bones meet.

ligament strong tissue that holds bones in place.

muscular system all of the muscles that cover the bones and move the body.

nerve a bundle of fibers that connects body parts and sends messages in the body.

nervous system the group of nerves and organs that control all activities in the body.

organ two or more tissues that work together to do a certain job.

organ system two or more organs that do a common task.

platelet a cell that stops bleeding by sticking together with other platelets to make a clot.

red blood cell a cell that carries oxygen from the lungs to the body tissues.

skeletal muscle muscle tissue attached to bones that works in pairs to move the body.

skeletal system the entire collection of bones and the tissues that hold them together in the body.

spinal cord a group of nerves that connect the brain with the rest of the body.

tendon a band of strong tissue that connects muscle to bone.

tissue a group of similar cells that do a certain job.

vertebrae a column of bones in the back that protect the spinal cord.

voluntary muscle a muscle that can be controlled by thinking.

white blood cell a cell that helps protect the body from diseases.

FIND OUT MORE

Books

Bones: Our Skeletal System
by Seymour Simon
(HarperCollins, 2000)

Bones: Skeletons and How They Work
by Steve Jenkins
(Scholastic Reference, 2010)

Human Body
by Richard Walker
(DK Children, 2009)

Human Body Factory: The Nuts and Bolts of Your Insides
by Dan Green
(Kingfisher, 2012)

Muscles: Our Muscular System
by Seymour Simon
(HarperCollins, 2000)

Start Exploring: Gray's Anatomy: A Fact-Filled Coloring Book
by Freddy Stark
(Running Press Kids, 2011)

The Bones Book and Skeleton
by Stephen Cumbaa
(Workman, 2006)

The Mighty Muscular and Skeletal Systems: How Do My Muscles and Bones Work?
by John Burstein
(Crabtree, 2009)

The Way We Work
by David Macaulay
(Houghton Mifflin/Walter Lorraine Books, 2008)

Websites

Biology 4 Kids: Skeletons Inside and Out
http://www.biology4kids.com/files/systems_skeletal.html
Get an in-depth education on all of the parts that make up the skeletal system.

Discovery Kids: Your Muscular System
http://kids.discovery.com/tell-me/science/body-systems/your-muscular-system
Get an in-depth education on all of the parts that make up the muscular system, fun facts included!

E-Learning for Kids: The Skeleton
http://www.e-learningforkids.org/Courses/Liquid_Animation/Body_Parts/Skeleton/
Take a peek inside your skeletal system in this clickable lesson with bonus comprehension exercises.

Kids Biology: Muscular System
http://www.kidsbiology.com/human_biology/muscles.php
Learn all about the muscular system by watching a short video and reading fact-filled articles complete with images of the body's muscles.

Kids Health: How the Body Works
http://kidshealth.org/kid/htbw/
Select a body part to watch a video, play a word find, or read an article to learn more about its function in the human body.

NeoK12: Skeletal System
http://www.neok12.com/Skeletal-System.htm
Watch videos that illustrate the inner workings of the skeletal system, and then take grade-specific quizzes to test your knowledge.

Science Kids: Human Body for Kids
http://www.sciencekids.co.nz/humanbody.html
Sample a range of educational games, challenging experiments, and mind-bending quizzes all while learning about human body topics.

INDEX